THIS NOTEBOOK BELONGS TO

Made in United States
Orlando, FL
27 May 2022

18252599R00068